PASSION AND COMMITMENT

THERESA J. WOLFWOOD

Passion and Commitment
Copyright © 2023 by Theresa J. Wolfwood
Front cover image: linocut by Oona Padgham
Published by:
Yalla Press
859 Maddison Street
Victoria BC V8S 4C3.
www.Yallapress.ca
yalla.press@yahoo.com
&
Smallberry Press
London
contact@smallberrypress.co.uk

First edition.
First published 2023.
10 9 8   7   6   5   4   3   2   1

ISBN
978-1-9992893-1-7 (Paperback)

Table of Contents

Passion and Commitment

Theresa J. Wolfwood

The wild side

I. As a girl
Innocent with no sense of fear, the girl
 liked to walk over the Fraser canyon,
high above the torrent
of dangerous water
 rushing to the sea.
with no parental knowledge or consent
 she and her dog, Perky,
 trekked the narrow boards, over the rail ties.
The CNR bridge arching
 from east to west was her secret path.
She, always tingled with anticipation,
hoping to see a cougar
or something else new and exciting:
Perky, not to be left at home, but
reluctant, was coaxed along the boards.
 The river roared so loudly
approaching trains were inaudible.
Engineers in the snorting steam
sounded the alarm; holding Perky,
she jumped onto a side platform,
waved as one hundred freight cars
rolled down to the Pacific.
Reaching the west side,
wild with no homes or roads,
dense bush coming close to the tracks,
deep in shadows;
she could see the east side, sun setting
 on homes, barns, roadside shops,
 trucks pulling on the gravel highway
to the north as she explored the hillside forest.

Before darkness the pair headed home
 so their absence would be unnoticed.
Back on the fields of grass and asparagus,
 Perky rushed to the orchard
 barking under trees filled with ghosts
 of long-gone bears, squirrels, birds.
In bed the girl dreamed of building
a log cabin, a secret retreat,
on the wild side.
Perky always curled up against her knees,
content with pursuit of never caught creatures.

II As an Adult

Decades later, far away,
 I dream the bridge of my childhood.
 I walked it again, silent,
 alone on the wild side.
No train disturbed my reverie.
Thinking of Perky, I feel her
warm against my legs in my dream.
The girl I once was, an outsider,
in a world with no place for
wandering girls and lone women.
I stood on the edge of the bridge,
looking across the still roaring river,
 into that world of commerce and community.
I saw you standing over there,
planted in the familiar comfort
of your garden in life. In my dream
I had to decide to walk towards you,
 hoping you might meet me halfway;
or if mine would be the long walk from
 the wild side to you.

The dream ended before I made my decision.
 I awakened filled with intense longing,
longing deeper than the canyon below
of fierce rapids and crashing rocks,
longing that you would find courage
 to walk across the chasm between us
to join me on the wild side

CNR bridge, Siska, British Columbia.

The Women I love

The women I love have dark skin, dread locks
that need not be dreaded, lips, ears,
noses pierced and be-ringed
to guard their gentle souls.
Some have stiff perms in grey-white hair,
crimped weekly under a blast of hot air;
they wear never-crease polyester sweaters, sensible
shoes and hesitant smiles.
Even those with tiny short skirts, impossible shoes,
yet able to stride the world
with needle nosed high heels, leading the way,
piercing tradition with armour of flash
 jewellery, lipstick and mascara,
maybe hidden tattoos.
 Some dress in hand spun skirts with metres
 of bright colours wrapped
around their compact bodies,
ribbons woven in their dark braids
bouncing on their backs.
Many wear denim pants of skin hugging tightness
with shrunk-to-cling T-shirts of dull shades,
scruffy boots.
There are women I love who throw
on the first garment
that comes to hand in the morning, rush to take up
keyboard and pen, song and music,
needle and thread,
 wooden spoon and pot, paint and brush, placards
and banners: I love their creativity, their resistance.
Some women I love wear hard hats
and wield chain saws: I love them

and those in fire-proof garb rushing to save
homes and lives with heavy high-pressure hoses.
And others I love cover their beautiful thick hair
with scarves elaborately pinned to stay put
 all day, draped down around over ankle length robes.
I love those whose saris are butterfly wings
with golden threads, ends fluttering,
flags as they walk confident of their identity.
I love those who walked so many miles,
 with heavy burdens, now immobile,
lying patient in pale gowns on narrow beds,
dependent on others whose needs they once served.
For women who were leaders, creative,
 active and beautiful, happy to see me.
I love also those who cannot yet walk,
yet smile and gurgle, wriggle in
diapers and cozy outfits of softest cloth.

I love them all for they are my sisters,
my children, engaged, but now are forgetful,
slow with muddled minds; I have a special love.
They are serene, my mothers.
They are me once past, maybe yet to be.

The Bedroom

Where the floor so polished
the black brogues are mirrored in the sunlight
beneath a dark suit
waiting after so many years
dated and unfashionable
as are the shoes
in this day of denim and white canvas.
For forty-one years lovingly brushed daily
as clothes wait to hang loose
on a shrunken frame when the prisoner returns
to rest on the smooth pink covered bed
to gaze out the window
at blue skies and olive trees.
Out the open gates into sunlight
where jubilant thousands crowd
to glimpse him, remember and rejoice
as he steps light footed on greeting ground
in those black shoes.
Gaunt in his dark suit he will be touched,
embraced, kissed to be loved again
after forty-one years.
Like freedom and peace
and steadfast hope fulfilled
never to see bars and
perpetual shades of grey again
to inhale the scent of za'atar
not the stench of human waste
to enter to leave as wishes
in a verdant land that knows no occupier.
Blessed to be called so many times every day-
not by a number but *Habibi* from the throats of
many   to taste the warm taboon bread

with zatoun oil,
to rest peacefully in this rose-tinted room,
his home in a land of fragrant love.

*Nael al-Barghouthi is Palestine's longest serving political
prisoner in Israel, He is 64 years old and has been in prison for
41 years. His wife, Nafi,, his family and friends await his
return.*

*World Press Photo by: Antonio Faccilongo,
an Italian documentary photographer,
winner of Foto Evidence Book Award*

The Bedroom (in Arabic)

ترجمة# :صالح_القاسم

أرضية غرفة النوم اللامعة

ذات التصليحات الواضحة

في ضوء الشمس

تنتظر منذ سنوات

صاحب البدلة السوداء

المعلقة

منذ سنوات عديدة

معلقة

مثل الأحذية في المحلات هذه الأيام

منذ واحد وأربعين سنة

تنظفها كل يوم

في انتظار عودة السجين

لتشاهد جلسته

على سريره الوردي

قبالة النافذة

يحدق في السماء والأشجار.

تشاهده وهو يخرج ويدخل من البوابات المفتوحة

تحت الشمس

آلاف سوف يحتشدون

لمشاهدته في فرح

وهو يخطو بزهو

على أرض الترحيب

بحذاء اسود

وبدلته الداكنة

سوف يعانقوه

ويغرقوه بالقبل

محبوبا مرة أخرى

بعد واحد وأربعين عاما

في حرية وسلام

أمل لا ينفد

في رؤية الحانات
والظلال الرمادية على الجدران
يستنشق رائحة الزعتر
لا رائحة الفضلات البشرية
يدخل ويغادر
الأرض الخضراء
دون محتل.
طوبى للدعوات
من حناجر الكثيرين
أن يدعوه يا حبيبي
لا رقما
ويتذوق خبز الطابون الساخن
المغمس بزيت الزيتون
في حب
هذه الغرفة المظللة بالورود
منزله
في ارض الحب الفواحة.

نائل البرغوثي: أقدم سجين سياسي فلسطيني في إسرائيل ، يبلغ #
من العمر 64 عامًا ويقبع في السجن منذ 41 عامًا. زوجته
ترجمة#: صالح_القاسم
كاتب وأديب اردني، شاعر وقاص ومترجم
تصوير: World P Press . نافع وأهله وأصدقاؤه ينتظرون عودته
Foto مصور وثائقي إيطالي ، حائز على جائزة ، Faccilongo
Evidence Book Award.

Memory

For Carole Chambers 1944-2014

1. **Time in the light**

There is time and also grace
to watch the kingfisher dive,
to find the first ripe blackberry;
or we will become like those
who love most of all
the echo of their own words,
the power of parliament,
the pomp of pulpit,
the thrill of screams
from fighter jets with their
deadly cargo, blessed
by those we elected
to rule in our interest,
who pray in a house of God
but cannot see the olives ripen,
children picking dandelion bouquets,
nor see the homeless slumped
in doorways. Politicians and priests
there is still time for you
to see the smallest seed
thrust up the thread of life,
hear a tree frog croak,
laughter in a playground,
see fir cones unfold, the tears
on a baby's shroud: Time still
to stop talking, see clouds become fruit,
to hear the earth, give voice to life.

ll. That Day

When the news came, I was eating cherries,
deep juices dripping from my mouth.
You died with a mouth full of blood
dripping your own juices;
unable for months to speak or
 to eat any food, but the day before
you wrote of grapes and love,
shared mouths joined in
passion and sweetness,
cherries and grapes
you will never savour again.
In every cherry I eat
you feed my soul.
Your never spoken words
fall from my mouth,
staining the page with love,
sweet moons of memory.

III. Ginger pots

In myriad variations of jade
they wait on your porch
shoulder to shoulder
your beloved ginger pots
squat and six-sided
with designs of unknown meaning
capped with flat stoneware lids
 you cherished each one as
you emptied it of candied ginger
chopped and folded into
cakes and cookies and
wait for your next visit

to Chinatown to stock up once more,
the day came when you were
 too frail to wander Fisgard Street,
so I went from store to store
until a clerk told me - not made
any more - ginger comes
in glass jars now from a factory
all sterile in their sameness
no quirks of the potter's brush
no squiggle of the symbols
no tints of sky in some
or sunlight in others.
I hold one of your many pots
rub its glowing sides
I wait for you to swirl out
in your garden green robes
to offer a plate of steaming cookies.

IV Your script

it begins with a wide-open C
open to the world of nature, art
 your E has reaching arms
to embrace with love precious people
and special places in the Salish Sea
every letter clear and important
every word you wrote a treasure
your poems, letters, recipes
written with strength and compassion
a world of understanding
your lower loops entangled
with tree roots
 bramble vines waiting seeds
your loops embrace around

hidden camas bulbs;
raven grasps your upper loops
pulls them away until your words
are scattered in the high firs
and cedars where raven
perches to defy the wind.
I open books and binders
your poem about Emily Carr
floats out, then a recipe
for quince compote
falls into waiting lap
now I call your partner Paul
the answering machine clicks on
I hear your voice, lilting like your writing
it promises to "get back to you"
Carole, you have never left me.

Tree and sea

the orchard floor covered with fruit
my grandson Géza and I marvel
as we bend to scoop up the blushing
crab apples, glowing in the rough grass
so easy in their redness waiting to be
found and to fill our boxes

we stand to look west down the hill
to the beach where waves
lap up dead crabs, red in their final stage
scorned by all except gulls
the fruit have no legs but bodies pinched
and curved like spent crustaceans.

we cherish the fruit softened and yielding
in its final stage a boiling
for jelly rendering a rich red juice
hard to accept that when death
strikes something so red in its prime
it is sweetest in its demise.

A poem about home

Home means my life of walls
covered with beloved art;
shelves of favourite books,
constant light and warmth,
a kitchen of familiar pots,
dishes, implements, cookbooks
to inspire great meals for friends.

Most of all the bed we share
our furrows of comfort,
of intersecting passion, blanketed
by warmth, safety, pleasure.
Tonight it is cold, windy, wet.
I rest in tranquility, happy in the glow.

I try to imagine no home. I think
of sloppy food on plastic plates;
street trees and neon signs for art.
In my cocoon I think about a damp
sleeping bag on a cold church floor,
maybe hidden under bushes in the park or
open to a world of abuse in some dry doorway.

Earth and cement are not mattresses.
A dirty pack is no pillow. For many
home is an unrequited dream.

The woman in the white coat

every time she comes
the manager seats her close
to the window facing out
she takes off her white coat
wears black underneath
an embroidered peasant style dress
fits in with the painted decor
and coloured lamps
she eats slowly waiting
for a man to enter
after seeing her alone
the Lorelei of Turkish
food and dinner talk
finishes with mint tea
and baklava
she leaves in her white coat
she has spoken only
to the friendly manager.

A fat white man exile

He lies on a Caribbean beach,
 has been there in exile
for years. He is still white
always shaded by an umbrella
protecting his skin.
He owes so many millions
in unpaid taxes that
he cannot go home.
He longs for smoky northern
sunsets, mosquitoes,
tamarack trees, the crisp note
of hammer on granite,
streaming caribou herds.
He sips his coconut drink and
stranded like a beached whale,
he can only brood that
he hates heat, palm trees,
green parrots that screech all day,
roosters that crow all night,
 and endless black sand,
endless more heat and parties;
 exiled forever by money he
cannot spend this side of a coral reef.

Sumoud is:

Setsuko as she takes the gift of years of life
to work for peace after surviving Hiroshima

Omar home from prison teaching his children
to read and to ignore the soldiers outside

Fatinatou baking love into her bread pours tea
with hope to leave this desert camp after 40 years

Gudrun still carrying a peace sign at 88 years
 hosting activists feeding friends tending her garden

Avi stitching the wounds of an injured
Palestinian - a secret from his colleagues-
sewing with the thread of compassion

Rosalie in pain, lungs and back collapsing as she
finishes one last paper on
the dangers of nuclear radiation

On a military runway grass pushes through
cracks in concrete as bombers screech
away loaded with their deadly gifts

Abu Ein without fear going with others to plant olive
tree dies choked and beaten,
leaves his spirit to his children

Rosita resisting torture by the dictator's soldiers
lives to laugh with her grand
children rejoice at her own sumoud

A stump of a giant old growth red cedar
now sprouting shoots for future
generations to marvel at

Gerd at 92 years frail and faltering goes to one last
vigil 70th anniversary
of the Hiroshima bomb sits in the sun

Sumoud makes us human as we live life with love

*Sumoud is the Arabic word for steadfastness: steadfast
perseverance, the quality most cherished in Palestine.*

Death with an olive tree

It was in December, a good time
to plant saplings in a land where
one million olive trees of every age
from 2000 years to two years old
have been stolen and destroyed
by a relentless purveyor of death.

When Ziad Aby Ain, fifty-five years old
 father and politician joined farmers
laden with small trees to plant
 on stolen land, he was beaten,
gassed, choked by armed soldiers
of a global power.
He died in the ambulance on a short trip
from Turmus Aya to Ramallah.
The world blinked and looked away.
No cabinet minister anywhere
stood for a moment of silence for
a parliamentary colleague.
No UN vote of censure;
no government sanctioned the invaders.

A lover of children and trees
mourned by his family, friends,
and the fragile olive tree that
died with him; he was cherished,
this good man, this good Palestinian.

About Virginia

What I enjoy most with Mom
 is going for our Sunday morning
walks in the country
among acres of farmland
wild roses lining the narrow road.

The sky looks so beautiful,
as the clouds can look so white and pillow soft.
We love watching the sheep, cows,
chickens and horses grazing in the fields
 the smell of fresh cut hay drying in the sun
or the scent of blackberries warmed by the sun.
 Sometimes we hear the odd rooster
cockle-a-doodling so loud and proud.

I listen to Mom reminisce about
 growing up in Monaco and England
and her horse riding in the country side
- stopping for lunch at an old English Pub:
the time she fell off her horse into a fence
when young doctor offered his assistance
- a near romance followed. Mom enjoys
talking about the horse and buggy rides in
Monaco by the waterfront with her father
- how he was very gentlemanly,
tipping his hat to passers-by. She was fascinated
watching fireflies at dusk. Mom loves talking about
the war days with her brothers, sisters,
 aunts and uncles; her memories
of close bonds she had with her family.

Based on a letter from Virginia's son

Night in the Negev

Soil and stone make
 an unkind mattress;
amidst the rubble of what was a house
no comfort can be found,
no shelter from knives of winter rain,
nowhere else to go; home they stay.

The family huddled for warmth;
children curled into each other
the smallest in the middle.
Dusty clothes layered on,
a few blankets retrieved from ruins,
plastic from a shattered greenhouse
kept the children dry.

Dry they were until soldiers came
and tore the plastic away;
their laughter muffled in the cutting rain.

Arctic spring

Annie crouched in the centre,
her family around, backs to the ice wall.
She wore an old amauti
its fur rubbed off with
holes in the hide;
she'd worn it for her marriage
and carried all her babies in it.

After each had chewed a bit
of fish while she waited,
they stood silent; she called out
I am Annie Arluk:
one by one they replied,
I am Jessie, daughter of Annie;
I am Simon, son of Annie;
I am Pudloo, Annie is like mother to me;
I am Aisa, Annie is my only mother.
The children slept:
Adamie, Gyta, Isa, Johnassie.
Annie bowed over
climb through the low door.
They watched silent again.
One dog worried a scrap of seal fur,
other dogs were rolled into balls
backs to raging south wind.
In the low fading light
Annie looked only ahead,
shuffling across bare patches
of dry lichen around dirty
mounds of old snow.
At sea's edge she pushed herself
forward as her kamiks slopped

in slush drenched water;
found her footing on a shifting ice flow.
Faced the wind and the falling sun
cross legged she sat and waited
under clouds driven to blind the stars
until spring's early dawn.
The ice flow was forced into the sea
into fog; Annie did not see
the promise of the rising sun.

Poem about spring

for Pablo Neruda

You wrote yours when our land was dying
into winter sleep, bereft of blossoms
 fruit picked, bletted. Our lands, our
latitudes, seasons apart; spring must travel
 from north to south to fulfill
 the promise of return with
warm winds and wild skies.
In our spring I think of you in
that time. September, your early spring
a time when promise was brutalized,
the blossoms of youth destroyed.
You were dying as your friends were massacred;
horrors you could never dream of were committed
to your companions in that cruelest of Aprils.

Yet spring returns as it always does.
 Eventually even cherries bloomed
and scarlet quince blossoms foretell
 the sweetness of fruit, the play of children;
lovers lie in carpets of blossoms
so red from the nurture of the blood of martyrs.
In sweet embrace lovers create universal spring
among swallows and tree frogs; soft earth
blooms and brings forth the fruit of another year.

Spring and its song makers:
music of sun and stars.

Waiting

She is waiting by the phone;
old-fashioned, a land line ties
her to the house.
She vows this is the last time,
not many years left
to fill with empty hours.
Life holds more than
an uncommitted lover
but yet, loneliness can kill.

Passion and Commitment

"Death must be earned" Jean Rhys

Sweat and blood are not enough.
They need passion to carry the cargo
on the long voyage, passion for justice,
passion for truth; even passion for beauty.

Commitment is the ticking of an old clock:
the turning of pages of calendars
 replaced every January;
years measured in tree rings.
Commitment is time, so slow to grow passion.
Passion can fade and wither without
seasons of care, climates of knowledge.
Commitment to peace, to love,
to justice, to that which cannot
be measured or defined.
The root, branch, the green
and blossom of passion
give lives of labour and struggle
the right to live on this
briefly borrowed planet.

When the load is too heavy to carry
as the pulse of passion diminishes;
accept with serenity, a kindness of reward.

Death earned with honour
and gratitude passes passion
and commitment to our heirs,
the earthworms of this world
we live and die for.

How far a bullet can travel

A soldier shoots a child
running frantic on the road
before her screaming in terror.
The bullet has an easy task
no fatigue, only ten metres to go
in a jungle village, a verdant land,
this place of peasants once happy
in belief of a certain god
who must now die for their faith.
The bullet has travelled
before it met the child, before
the gun fired in instant readiness.
The bullet travelled on an airplane,
accompanied by so many others
identical in form and purpose
from a factory in the distant desert
near Galilee, a land of another god,
a land that loves death.
Bullets by millions - all the same.
That child was only one
unique   beloved
no factory can replace her.

Dora's Christmas

Waking early to catch the hen
she'd been plumping up,
Dora loves the cool of the morning,
banana plants rustle and
scrape their leaves together;
small tits swoop in flocks for scraps,
the chickens cluck in their coop,
they have eaten grain and
produced the miracles of eggs.
Children awaken one by one,
they are excited waiting for miracles,
chores are done, the hen is plucked,
corn freshly ground,
vegetables dug and cleaned.
After the meal the children
play with their gifts,
two brightly coloured balls.
Dora's husband surprises her
with a shiny red scarf.
Church and visits to family nearby,
the day ends with contentment and gratitude.
Dora lies resting her swollen belly,
twisting the red scarf
through her bare bony fingers -
no gold ring for her; children
are more precious than any metal.
she dreams of names-
for a girl- Maria, after her mother,
if another boy- maybe Jesus will suit.

Next day life continues as
Dora takes her laundry to the river,

THERESA J. WOLFWOOD

little Jose on her hip
plays with a box of soap.
Along a worn path
to the sweet sound of running
water to her favourite pool,
water so clear she can see
each grain of sand
glistening beneath her feet.
Downstream are other women
bathing and washing as children
shriek in their splashing games;
laughter fills this cathedral of green,
flowers, stones, rippling water.

When the water starts flowing red
the women creep silently upstream
to find Jose blooded and crying
clinging to his mother washed
pale and still against a ring of rock,
her shiny red scarf impaled on a root.
One silenced shot from nearby bushes
Dora's day   Dora's life is over.
Friends weep with the child,
they carry Dora's body and Jose
back to her family.

As the river flows to the sea
resistance flows stronger
to never let sacrificed blood
nor cyanide slurry obscure
the glistening sands of Rio Titiguapa.

Dora Alicia Sorto Recinos, 32, was shot and killed December 27, 2009. She was eight months pregnant. Her son, who was accompanying her, was shot in the foot.

She was a community activist trying to preserve the local clean water and environment when a Canadian mining company wanted to develop an operation that would contaminate the water and soil. She is one of four who were assassinated for their protective activism. El Salvador now bans metal mining and won a trade agreement challenge by this mining company.

Holding onto a Wall

Walking the Great Wall of China
feet gripping the toughest of stones,
hands on a fragile rail, we climbed
a wall, really a highway
for unforeseen journeys.
It is wide enough for
chariots of war to patrol
constant watch for enemies.
Its unforgiving hardness
I endured for hours it seemed.
On the train back to Beijing-
the number One train for tourists-
for relief we drank Mau Tai
of terrible taste and strength
unknown to foreign visitors.
Emboldened by its effect
the kind man cradled my feet
in his lap massaged away the soreness.
After that we were inseparable
through meals, museums, more,
until the night I cradled him in my arms.
I tried to relieve his pain but no power,
my love or even a greater power,
could hold him back from his fate.
I continue the journey alone.

I listen to the wind

Alone in my big house
still in my warm bed
I can hear the wind,
strong from Arctic darkness
it comes in heavy breaths
it moans with
pauses of silence like
the silence between notes
in a Beethoven concerto.
Each time I hold my breath
expecting an end or change,
so constant in this world around me.
 I sleep before the roaring ceases,
wake up in sunlight to see
the litter of broken fir branches
and wait for another night to lie
alone with only the wind.

Charity

Faith and hope are a piece of cake but charity is a Pandora's box...True charity...consists in swallowing an invisible flaming sword.
From: Allen Bradley in: *Thrice the Brindle Cat hath mew'd.*

We think we are being kind:
poor soul does not know any better,
had a dysfunctional family life,
as they say now- but
meaning alcoholism, misery, poverty,
probably domestic violence.

We had privileges, so
from that vantage pinnacle
of glowing well-being, we look
down and feel not charity but pity.
The most contemptible of emotions
—can only inflate our sense of superiority.

Nothing changes for that person. We go
on with our separate lanes on life's race track;
we sprint along in the sunlight,
aflame in momentary glory.
She falls and limps along,
lost in the inevitable darkness.

Parallel Tracks

Beside the station banks
of shrubs and flowers are
alive with the buzz of bees
in spring blossoms.

Below the foot bridge
two sets of parallel tracks
slice through a Scottish postcard scene.
Closer to the platform tracks
gleam in the watery sun,
well worn and polished
by constant use. They
carry the life blood
of this idyllic rural place;
workers to jobs,
students to school,
some to medical
appointments in the city,
shopping, art galleries,
meeting friends via
a major artery streaming
silver in the sun.

Close by, never touching
a pair of rusty racks, lie
seemingly abandoned,
unused; but in quiet hours
it moves deadly cargo;
nuclear missiles shifted
from military base to factory
for renewal as uranium
atoms fright against containment;

and spent rods from
leaky power plants to
destinations unknown.
There is readiness every moment
for the message of a distant button
pressed by one man
allowed to destroy life;
to decree an end to human history.
Rust lies on these tracks
but never stops
the silent containers, closed to view
and knowledge.Like lines
of invisible latitude
these rails track the world.
They are radiating and criss-crossing
life everywhere as babies
are born and tomatoes ripen red,
from Faslane to Nanoose;
Nevada to Gorlaben;
Marshall Islands to Okinawa;
Galilee to Semipalatinsk,
atoms never sleep or cease their travail.

One journey only we have
on this earth; we have choice.
We can choose unnatural death
on rusty rails for all creation
or choose life so that all may live.
Life thrives there on sunlit tracks.
We will determine our future.

A full moon

A full moon fell through my window
came to rest on the kitchen table,
became a plate laden with
truffles in risotto, roasted
chestnuts, honey, chocolate.
We ate our fill
and went out to walk
the moon was smiling
above us as
it fell into a halo
around your face,
my cold head was warmed
by a magic white beret
that landed like a nest of
feathers on my dark hair.

When we came home
the moon entered our bed
and was transformed into
my belly, so smooth and firm
your hands caressing the roundness
with fires of love until
darkness enfolded us.
The moon slipped away
to light other lovers.

The Day after Washing Day

When she sings, hope trembles
in high notes as she irons
his shirts with a heavy
clumsy instrument heated
on the wood stove.
Three wedges take their turns,
one works while two reheat.
She sighs and wonders
how she got here
in the Canadian bush
with a man who still
wants crisp creases
in the sleeves
of white shirts.
The child plays
on the floor
with letter blocks;
she feels sad for
her mother but
does not know why.

Welcome to this home

Welcome to this home
where arms are open
to greet you, where
hearts enfold you in love.
May the bounty
of food and friendship
nourish us all in spirit and body.
When we part may we
remember this circle
of companions; may we
be forever together
in spirit and compassion;
holding fast in our lives
of committed love.
For now, we meet to share
food by the fire and
be held in the warmth
of flame and friends.

So many of us are scientists

So many of us are scientists.
We practise the formulae,
create the algorithms,
use theories.
We measure lives
in numbers of objects;
yet we dwell in words
of deep understanding,
we lay poems on a page
to express our longings,
to tell our loves and fears.
Infinity cannot be contained,
controlled or confined
by science. Scientists
become poets to break
science's limits; only words surge
through us, rushing
to the life of creativity,
of contemplation,
of compassion.

With Ann on the Amazon

The night you died
I dreamed
you and I were floating
down the Amazon.
 A friendly safe Amazon-
no piranhas, crocodiles
 or biting insects. We were
carried in bliss
by colourful bird song.

In soft sunlight we rested on a
wide raft, dry although
our hair streamed silver in
the silver waters.

We drifted along as tributaries
poured in memories;
our last talk about love,
 shared times, secrets.

Our talk over,
 no need for words,
the river carried us out to sea;
 silently, fingers intertwined,
we floated on to Palestine.

September Equinox

A doe, two fawns and
two bucks inhabited my garden
on the day of equinox.
Hungry and curious,
they ignored holly
and bay, too tough and sharp;
rejected geranium and herbs,
their scent not pleasing.
Awkward on the rocky
edges of my hill,
they balanced between
summer and winter,
seeking English roses, apples,
ripe tomatoes. They snapped
instead, orange lilies from Peru,
next year's raspberry growth,
nibbled blueberry bushes beside
Japanese maples. Between hunger
and taste they sampled and stumbled
until they wandered off to investigate
the neighbour's offerings.
Not easy to find balance
between night and day,
territory and need, changing seasons.
My global garden fenced and protected,
was once a native wilderness,
a sanctuary in all seasons.

Widows

My friend told me about
 a survey of widows.
They all said they
did not experience ageism.
No one called them 'dear', cheated
them on their home repairs, or
pushed by them in crowded shops.
They were all in their 80s and 90s
but denied knowing discrimination.

Also, they loved their new lives-
eating when and how they wanted,
going anywhere anytime
to places of their own choice.
They liked to spend money
without control or censor.

They did not mention hours alone,
their fear of dying during sickness
or after injury, usually a fall at home;
occupying only one side of a large bed.
No one to tell them they looked great
after zipping up a new dress or to kiss
 bare shoulders imbued
with his favourite perfume.

These widows forget the dark hours
when many lives go on without love;
when silence falls from
the undented pillow
on the other side of the bed.

The Lovely House

White outside, white inside,
glossy leather chairs,
chrome and glass tables.
Impossible to allow mess,
unable to tolerate it.
No children to spill food or drink:
white carpet remains pristine.
Kitchen is so sterile so clean,
no one else can use it;
easier to take friends out to eat.
State of art sound system makes
noise to fill the motionless air.
The house remains impeccable;
sheltered in hedges and trees,
lovely in its perfection of self-gratification.

From London to Bangor

"Life can only be understood backwards,
but must be lived forward" Soren Kierkegaard

Dark red brick walls
where buddleia
bursts the mortar
and droops pale blossoms
on steel rails below; where
'Live carelessly' is scratched
in white chalk under the
persistent stem.

Later beyond random homes,
warehouses, shops, car lots,
a willow sprouts upward,
I see the flash of
painted words beneath
naming it the 'tree of life'.

Then canals crossing wide
valleys on high bridges,
narrow boats
in parking ponds
awaiting a couple to lie
languid in love; docked
under curtains
of leafy tendrils.

Seated backwards
I see clearly
what is past in this land

of impossibly few vowels,
gentle greens
of countless sheep.

Only yesterday
I learned that death
is the release of love.

Birth Blanket

The clouds gave me a blanket,
sky blue and lined with love,
wrapped me into it
 when I was born.
Holes appear when
I lose someone
Carol left a hole this week;
holes begin to merge.
Soon I will be bare,
cold and unprotected.
Then as all those souls
gone like clouds
before me,
I will disappear.

Abandoned

Past a wide swath of lupins,
we started our way home
away from the busy highway.
We walked between the rusted rails,
fishplates and square sided spikes
fallen from once active duty,
scatter between the weeds and
grass pushing into prominence.
Moss growing in some old
ties make earth
for sharp gravel cutting
the grain of sturdy fir;
some ties rotted totally away;
their furrow now a tree nursery.
Above maples and alders
arch over, softening sun light
and air wafts wild rose scent.
Briars and blackberry
creep up the rocky banks.
We pause to hear rustling and twigs
cracking in the dense bush-
we are not alone
in this wild community.
Songbirds unseen
in full voice enter the silence.
These rails once shone
and hummed with use;
wood and iron held the force
of freight and people
moving up and down
our forested island.
Bridges and trestles are

neglected into dangerous decay,
unable to support any traffic.
We reach the next crossroad,
signal boxes and road signs
remember a time of purpose.
Too soon we are on the highway
as vehicles small and huge
spew fumes and roar to serve
with speed society's desires.

*The Esquimalt and Nanaimo Railroad
was a condition of BC joining Canada
but has been abandoned and left
to deteriorate. Photo by CAA.*

The key and the labyrinth

My dear friend came to visit,
only now can I say to her
thanks for your generous creativity,
your sharp humour bounces off mine.
Together we laugh a lot.
I admire your productivity, your persistence,
you support my efforts, you came to
read from your new book, to encourage
reluctant writers like me.

You looked at my photo of
a Palestinian refugee camp in Jordan -
a mottled wall with a carefully lined map
that familiar elusive wedge shape
with words, bold in urgent Arabic,
that say: we shall return.
You sat down not noticing
my antique dress from Ramallah
hanging beside your chair, firmly
you said: they won't you know.

I responded: I do not know but
many people think otherwise.
You demanded: would you hold on
to an old house key for sixty years?
I ponder your question friend of fifty years;
we have walked many roads together,
our differences must not cleave our friendship.

I reply: I am not Songhees,
born to salmon and cedar,
· nor Dene of black spruce and cold granite;

not an indigenous person who lives
where my grandparents and theirs lived
before them. I cannot breathe
the air from familiar soil
that holds my unknown ancestors
in many distant grounds.
Nor am I of the land of olives and palms,
of spice caves and taboun ovens,
I am not a Palestinian who has never been home.
So, I cannot answer your question.
I do not claim any land, I result from restless
conquerors, of generations who scattered their seed
and bullets around the planet carelessly,
born on one continent to breath on many.

The next day we walk the labyrinth
on a chapel floor, a map of clear green lines
curving on new clean canvas
 geography easy to roll up and store,
 a world without roots or blood.
In silence we pass one another
converge, brush sleeves, diverge until
we meet in the key shaped hearth.

Your question unanswered
forces us apart, on this shallow world
like the school map where our
empire was always in red, our empire,
even Palestine, was coloured
the red of blood and soil before
 we were born randomly anywhere.
A rusty key stains its wrap of crumbling canvas;
now it may not open any door,
unable to greet its memories, to know its rooms.

While we stand together silent in the hearth
within the key shaped centre of this
flimsy labyrinth which could be anywhere;
we leave no trace of our entry
or our twisted journey.

We go in wordless heavy silence
into magnolia scented air,
walk down the hasp shaped exit,
free to go where we please, never exiled from
the world of conquest we inherited.
I do not answer your question
but it hovers waiting under the firs
and cedars of our strolling.

It really matters not that I do not have
the key to a door a grandfather carved
or for a home filled with the perfume
of grandmother's bread fresh from the taboun.
It matters for you that you cling to the trunk and its key
of your grandmother's voyage.
She, an orphan girl, sent to work for harsh employers
in a cold colony, you wrote her story,
keeping her key close by to inspire you.
It matters that somewhere many have faith,
have strength to hold on, inspired by a key.

My answer is to depart this indulgent
turning on myself; instead I choose to
walk that line on the camp wall with
the dispossessed toward
their waiting locks
to open forgotten doors.
I too have faith in keys,

I banish not courage or hope.
but the false labyrinth of desperate power.
I dream to reunite the living
with their land and their dead.

Until

A glossa variation based on the chorus of the song by Judy Small: on the CD "Never turning back" produced by Crafty Maid Music, Australia

"Until the swords turn into plowshares
Until the children eat their fill
Until the mansions admit the lowly
We have no cause to stand still"

With the roar of guns, the screams of women,
armament profits soar with every conflict:
until rape as a weapon of war ceases, we shall cry out
until swords turn into plowshares.

They come to school without breakfast, cold
inadequate clothes, sleepy and sick
in the land of plenty and wealth; we shall cry out
until the children eat their fill.

Young people shiver on Pandora Street where
buildings are empty; church basements are cold and
dark. We turn away, drive by,
we will cry out
until the mansions admit the lowly.

There is beauty in the world, soft voices of peace,
snowdrops and cherry blossoms. Mozart's music
cannot drown out the call for justice, until then
we have no cause to stand still.

Dancing on Death

They came
women by the dozens
then women by hundreds
more women came by thousands
until thirty thousand joined hands
to embrace the base at Greenham
Common RAF base storge for USA
nuclear weapons designed to kill life
women cut wire fences by hand climbed
on ladders and by foot they gathered on
the silos of death they held hands danced
on earth and concrete as their feet sounded
like heart beats of babies- united in voice like
songbirds until their music rose in a sky full of
ascending larks with music enough to stop the
war planes from descending to collect their deadly
loads so women stayed until the weapons were
gone as they danced their final dance of power
of life's peace the music that rises
from hope and action
women embrace
everywhere
dance more powerful
than any politician's death wish.

Lunch with a friend

We meet in a local cafe for lunch -
you never forget a meal date; you
fill your lonely hours with a few friends.
Over cold coffee you recount the tales
of wealthy ancestors of homes with servants
far away and your schoolteacher father's discipline.

Yet again, you revisit old landscapes
while your signposts all
point inward to where fog streams over
old memories in African colours.
You trace a bread crumb
in ever decreasing spirals
on an empty plate once
a world traveller; when I take you to a shop nearby
you have forgotten what you wanted there.
When your mental mists clear
the present is full of angry words -
Canada geese, anchored boats,
drivers who drive as badly
as you once did - all incur
your disapproval, you harp
on imagined slights,
criticize caring friends, reject conciliation,
 get lost in parking lots yet stay in sightlines of home.
Downtown has become fearful geography.
Your shattered compass swings from
indignation and malice to sentimentality.
 You cultivate your personal wars;
once you were a woman of peace.

Snakeskin in the path

It lies between blades of grass
brittle in its lightness,
grass glowing around and under it.
When I shed my skin of
doubt and fear I see the pushing out
of hyacinth spikes
through my brittleness.
My life's hours in a casement
of overlapping translucent scales,
perfect and precise even in its final hour.
Grass is a good home for vanquished
fears on a traceless path well walked
at the end of a journey.

Still Breathing in Gaza

The Shifa hospital morgue over-flowing,
bodies in blood-soaked white shrouds
blanket entire floor space.
Some are intact,
most horribly deformed, limbs twisted
into unnatural positions,
chest cavities exposed, heads blown off,
skulls crushed in.
Families cling together in hope, yet
wait in fear to identify and claim a brother,
husband, father, mother, wife, child.
They have been here before.

Blood is everywhere. Hospital orderlies
hose down the floors of operating
rooms, bloodied bandages lie discarded
in corners; the injured still pour in bodies
lacerated by shrapnel, burns, bullet wounds.
Exhausted and in constant danger
medical workers work unceasingly
each life saved a victory
over the dominance of death.

Our streets are eerie in the silence
the pulsing life and rhythm of
markets, children, fishermen walking down
to the sea at dawn brutally stilled
stolen by an atmosphere
of uncertainty, isolation and terror.
Ever-present sounds of surveillance drones,
F16s, tanks and Apaches
are heard with acute fear.

Residents try to guess where the next deadly
strike will be; which house, school, clinic,
mosque, governmental building
or community centre will be hit,
how to move before it does.
There are no safe places, no refuge for
vulnerable human bodies: parents aware,
there is no way to keep their children safe.

Ambulance drivers, medics, paramedics
risk their lives, respond to those with no
other lifeline; our existence becomes
narrow, we focus on the few precious minutes
that make the difference between life
and death. At each call received we cling inside
ambulances that careen down broken, silent roads,
sirens and lights blaring, wherever
there exists a battle of life over death.

We have learned the language
of the war that Israelis wage;
the collective captive population of Gaza
can distinguish between the sounds
of the weaponry used,
the timing between the first missile strikes
and the inevitable second that targets those
who rush to tend and evacuate the wounded,
to recognize the dreaded signs of
different chemical weapons,
to overcome our initial vulnerability
as we recognize our mortality.

Many calls received are to pick up bodies,

not only the wounded,
the necessity of affording the dead
a dignified burial forces paramedic
to recognize deliberate targeting
of their colleagues and comrades,
thirteen killed while evacuating the wounded,
fourteen ambulances destroyed,
yet we continue to search for shattered bodies
of the dead to bring home to their families.
Not breathing in Gaza.

Last night, in Jabaliya refugee camp,
drinking tea and listening to stories, we are called
to respond to the aftermath of a missile strike.
We arrived to see the place in clouds of dust,
torn electricity lines, slabs of concrete,
open water pipes gushing water into the street.
Amongst the carnage of severed limbs and
blood we pulled out the body of a young man,
his chest and face lacerated by shrapnel wounds,
conscious, moaning and still breathing.

The ambulance sped him through the cold night
as we applied pressure to his wounds,
warm blood seeping through the
bandages remind of the life still in him.
He opened his eyes, closed them as Muhammud,
a volunteer paramedic, murmured *ayeesh, nufuss*
- live, breathe, live breath -- over and over to him.
We arrived at the hospital; his unconscious body
received by friends who carry
him into the emergency room.
Still breathing in Gaza, Majid lived.

Another missile strike, on a home. A crowd
rushed to the ruins, attempted to drag
survivors rom under the rubble.
The family had evacuated the area the day before,
seventeen-year-old Muhammud had returned
to collect clothes for his family. He was dragged
from the rubble, his legs twisted in unnatural
directions, with a head wound, but alive.
We had to move him, before a possible second
strike.   In the ambulance he moaned with pain,
called for his mother, still breathing in Gaza.

We thought he would live, he was conscious
though in intense pain. This morning
we were called to collect a body
from Shifa hospital, a body wrapped
in a blood-soaked white shroud. It was Muhammud.
His brother rode with us, opening the shroud to
tenderly kiss Muhammud's forehead.
Not breathing in Gaza.

Today Al-Quds hospital in Gaza City is under
siege. We tried to gain access to the hospital,
to organize co-ordination to get
the ambulances past Israeli tanks
and snipers to evacuate the wounded and dead.
Hours of unsuccessful attempts later
a call from the Shujahiya neighborhood,
describing a house; dead and wounded patients to
pick up. The area was deserted, many families had
fled when Israeli tanks and snipers took up position
amongst their homes, other silent in the dark,
cold confines of their homes, crawl from room to
room to avoid snipers' ire through their windows.

As we drove, we heard women's cries for help.
We stopped, approached on foot, followed by the
ambulances, we came to the threshold of their home,
they rushed towards us with their
children, shaking and crying with shock.
Ambulance lights exposed the bodies of four men,
lacerated by shrapnel wounds, the skull and
brains of one exposed, others with severed limbs.
They were husbands and brothers of the women,
who had ventured out to search for food for their
families. Their bodies still warm as we carry them on
stretchers over the uneven ground, their blood stains
earth, our clothes. Torches illuminated the slumped
figure of another man, his abdomen and chest
shredded by shrapnel. We had to put his body in the
back of the ambulance carrying the women and
children. One of the little girls stared at me before
coming into my arms, tells me her name- Fidaa,
which means to sacrifice. She stared at the body bag,
asking when he would wake up.
Not breathing in Gaza.

Once back at the hospital we received word
the Israeli army had shelled Al Quds hospital,
the ensuing fire risked was spreading, we had
20-minute timeframe to evacuate patients, doctors
and residents nearby. Our convoy of ambulances
joins hundreds of people. After the shelling
of the UNRWA compound and the hospital came
deep awareness: nowhere in Gaza is safe, or
sacred.   Still breathing in Gaza.

Helped evacuate those assembled
to near-by hospitals and schools opened
to receive the displaced. Families, desperate, carry
their children, blankets, bags of their possessions
into the cold night, try to find a
corner of a school or hospital for shelter.
The paramedic said this displacement of fifty
thousand Gaza Palestinians was a continuation of the
ongoing Nakba of dispossession and exile
seen through generation after generation
enduring massacre after massacre.

Today's death toll was over seventy-five,
one of the bloodiest days. The humanitarian
infrastructure of Gaza is on its knees- already
devastated by years of comprehensive siege.
There has been a deliberate, systematic destruction
of all places of refuge. There are no safe places here,
for anyone. In the face of so much desecration,
this community has remained intact.
The social solidarity and support between people
inspires us.   Still breathing in Gaza.

The steadfastness of Gaza continues to humble all
who witness it. Their level of sacrifice demands
our collective response and recognition.
Demonstrations are not enough. Gaza, Palestine,
its people continue to live, resist and remain intact
this refusal to be broken is a call and challenge to us
all.   Still breathing in Gaza.

A poem based on a letter "Still Breathing, A Report from Gaza" from Caoimhe
Butterly, an Irish human rights activist working in Jabaliya and Gaza City as a
volunteer with ambulance services and as co-coordinator for the Free Gaza
Movement, She can be contacted on 00972-598273960 or at
sahara78@hotmail.co.uk

Tomatoes and the news

Their lifelines are pale tendrils
That thread through soil
densely packed ready to expand;
spring and time to plant.
Seedlings grew from dry seed
that carried life long after
my friend Valerie's death

I remember her as
I cosset her tomatoes,
listen to music on the radio.
She was a consummate gardener,
faithful to the seasons,
to the lexigraphy of vegetables
and loyal to her friends.
The old Russian man who gave
her seed his father brought
from the old country in the lining
of his shabby sheepskin coat

She said they were sturdy,
not pretty, rough shaped
with strong ribs red
with paler red flesh,
but dense and meaty.

They bear every year
from my saves seed and
I know about the Russian man,
but it is Val's voice I hear

manure, sunlight, compost
lots of water.
 I follow her voice clearly
though she fell with a stroke
fifteen springs ago,
in a garden shop,
looking for a new shovel.

What comes in the night

the crash of a door broken down
boots clump on wooden floors
up the stairs, vases crash, the cat howls.
some glide on slipper soft feet
only the slight creak of a hinge
you hear nothing until
the cold click of the safety catch
dark walls, closed shutters,
warmth of sheets are but a trap
for the ease of the hunter.

Swans on the Peace River

From the white flames of mist
a pair of angel birds emerges,
glowing in the early light,
life partners side by side
they glide to stands of grass;
the Peace River flows
steady and gentle
as they paddle in effortless
unison grazing the surface
with heads down.
They stop from time to time,
entwine their arched necks
to nibble each other's feathers:
behold their beauty.

For Dane-zaa people
they are the symbol,
sacred totem,
of enduring faith and hope.
As long as this river flows,
swans will nest and bring
forth their young.
A dammed river does not flow:
 swans will vanish into eternal mist
with the hope and faith
of a betrayed people.
Then the lament of the Dane-zaa
will be the swansong of all.

Riding the Bloor Line

Above the ground,
the cold of Toronto;
minus twenty and windy.
Below in another world
of darkness and strange lights
the Bloor Line tunnels
from Ossington to Danforth.

The heat of steel wheels
on steel rails makes the trains
around zero inside, a bit warmer.
Sitting on cold plastic seats
grateful for all many layers,
heavy boots, I sat across
from a huddled man in
a flimsy wind cheater,
the hood pulled over his face.
I could not see his skin or eyes
but he looked young.
His knuckled hands clasped
together on his boney knees
sharply poking through
the thin fabric of his trousers.
Averting my eyes
not wanting to embarrasses
I looked down at his feet,
bare, toes hanging over in
half-broken flip-flops.
He was still motionless
in his huddle when
I got off wondering

if he would ride the tunnel
under a colder city all day,
because it was the warmest place
he could sit undisturbed.
Finally having to leave to walk
skin on ice and snow,
bonding together
on a perpetually wounded earth.

It is there

In Hell
a special
place is
reserved
 for those
who design
airport
furniture.

It is also there

In deepest
Hell
a place held
 for those
who
design
airplane
seats.

In Entebbe Airport

Checking in, the official looking at my passport
said: we have the same birthday;
 I see hundreds of passports; you are first to be
born same day as me. She whisked me into a short
 line, but computer was slow-slow.
She gave me a chair to sit in beside the desk;
then computer was down-down.
We chatted until an hour later, it worked again.
I kissed my bags farewell for the next four flights.
They were smiling at me in Victoria when I arrived.
Back in Entebbe I was surrounded
by a flutter of young women like
butterflies in blue pants
 and smart white blouses with a corporate logo.
Vibrating nervous energy they checked in,
each with only a piece of carry-on.
I joined them on hard benches and questioned them.
A sturdy moon-faced girl spoke up: We are going
with this company as maids to Saudi Arabia.
Years of stories of abuse flooded my mind,
showed in my face. She told me we stay in a hostel;
we only work in homes during daytime. There is not
work in Uganda. After two years
I can buy land, be a farmer; that is all I know.
I am not afraid, we will be together, we will be OK.
The flight was announced. The woman
across from us put her white-scarfed head
between her knees and sobbed silently.

Watching the end

When our world ends
surely soon in
the near future,
an end created by human
ingenuity harnessed to iniquity.

People will be clamped to
their hand-held devices
watching the end arrive
somewhere else.
So intent they will not
be conscious of
their own impending end
until it paralyzes them
 with their fingers
crooked alert
thumbs poised
frozen over
a blackened screen.

From blue barrettes to orange shirts

The girls clustered in the toilet
beside the rusty sink
with the cold tap dripping;
under a small broken mirror.
The girls whispered quickly
to each other ignoring
the stench from
the trough that carried
waste and disinfectant
flushed out daily.
I can smell it now
in the back of my nostrils.
Mary showed off her
new barrettes, her pair of bows;
one in pink said
YES in black letters:
the other in blue said NO.
Mary spoke out, they don't like them
but I'll wear them anyhow.
Marie defiant, agreed,
I will wear mine too.
Another Mary in tears added
I am afraid to wear mine now,
I got bawled out; I wonder why.
Josephine, the smallest of all,
with an owl-wise face
too old for her so tiny body,
she could barely see into
into the fragment
of mottled mirror,
whispered softly,

they don't like the blue one,
they don't like it
when we say NO.
When the bell clanged
the girls dispersed
and scuttled away.

Years later, my mother and I
heard on the radio the bishop
of our church diocese
had gone to prison.
The same bishop who confirmed
my sister and me was guilty
of sexually abusing girls
in a residential school.
We sat silent in horror
until my mother said: to think I had
that despicable man in my home.
while I thought of Josephine.

The call came from Unistoten women
Send red dresses, many are needed.
We want to hang them
along the pipeline route,
the pipeline that goes
though our traditional land.
Red dresses, symbols of
wise elder women, become
symbols of so many
murdered and missing
women and girls.
Anywhere near a man-camp
they are not safe; pipelines,
mines, dams, highway construction,

where men freed from social
restriction, full of lust, do
their foul deeds, then tear
the dresses from the trees.
Red dresses now are everywhere,
on my city street, waving beside
country roads and lining church walls,
messages we can no longer ignore.
They speak on the wind:
No more murdered and missing
indigenous women and girls.

A little girl named Phyllis had to go,
her parents were ordered,
they had no choice.
They gave her new clothes,
including an orange shirt.
The first day at the residential school
on September 30, her new clothes
were taken from her.
Years later when a mature woman
Phyllis told her story; September 30
became the day to remember
all those who were dragged away
from family, community, culture.
They were incarcerated
in ugly buildings whose thick walls
deafened cries and screams
form the world. We remember
together in shame, horror and love.

This year news shocked
but did not surprise;
215 children's bodies found

in unmarked graves beside
a closed residential school.
Grief and anger ask: Where are
the missing ten thousand
who never came home?
The steps of our settler
government building are covered
with symbols of lost childhood,
stuffed teddy bears, tiny shoes,
small shirts; 215 orange T-shirts,
lovingly arranged, fading in the sun.
But I can see on them
in bold black letters: Every child mattress.
I stand silent and think of Josephine.

*St. George Residential School, Lytton, BC photo
from internet (destroyed by 1st Nations to create
a housing development about 20 years ago)*

Orange shirts are now worn by survivors and supporters.
So many designed, so many stories from cultures
that could not be extinguished, grace these shirts. BC
Legislature, Victoria BC, July 2021. Photos by CAA.

Red dresses, Victoria BC. Photos by CAA.

Willow

When I first t visited
the willow in your garden
was coming alive
with tiny baby fingernails uncurling
yellow as the spring sun.

Ove the weeks the air was clear
dust motes glittered
still and silent like time
nothing moved
as the world was stopped
in its relentless destruction
by a small molecule of protein
designed to confound
the might of the mightiest
and to stop the cosmic clocks.

Minutes and seconds
days and hours
pas without notice
yet the weeks pass as
motes wait for signals
hanging in the air
the willow leaves
become baby fingers
of green curling crowding
down the slender branches.

In the hiatus love
became alive everywhere
the new growth
brought hope to the desparate
water to the thirsty
meaning to the lonely
new purpose to power
and compassion to many who
may ever have known it.

Love in a parking lot

They walked slowly, a tall white-haired man
one would expect to stride his pace;
He held the hand of a small frail grey haired
woman, erect but stepping with care
on the uneven gravel.
He measured his pace, to only
the length of his feet to match her short steps.
Held tight to her hand, bent his head,
not only to listen to her every word;
also to watch her move without falter.
They reached the door,
up the stairs hand in hand.
I watched them from my car
 and joined them for the concert.
I knew their love was
deep without boundaries,
not confined to a walk in a parking lot.

Gernika

A postcard town,
homes and trees aligned on a valley slope;
a vision of peace and prosperity.
Street signs in two languages;
laughing citizens greet strangers in open cafes.
Beauty that hides history. On April 26 1937
children leaving school, meals simmering in kitchens,
workers walking home, fruit trees in bloom.
The Gernika oaks in fresh leaf,
shelter of democracy where citizens met
to govern under the loveliest of greens,
when Operation Rügen hailed
 its horror, a gift to Franco from friends
Hitler and Mussolini,
devastation from a clear sky,
unknown until this day
which changed forever
the nature of warfare.
Explosions ripped
the bodies of thousands;
rubble was the ultimate gift
 in the remains of Gernika.
Left standing by design,
beside the river,
an ugly gray building, an arms factory
to serve Franco, later Japan,
then Morocco's war on the Saharawi,
a factory where silenced workers
created death on assembly lines.
I saw this building still standing;
now with a tower of colour
and peace as an entry portal.

Gernika reclaimed this place,
exorcized the evil,
transformed it to a community
centre where peace conferences
meet, children play,
creativity for all is nurtured.
Gernika in all its beauty reclaimed.

In a Mexican Café

A small café sky light high above
in an old entry hall
of an apartment house,
a young woman,
 pretty in a quiet way,
sat, silently crying.
Her tears were steady
streams on her soft cheeks
She was near us,
 only four tables in all,
she sat by a blue tiled
sink with plants and
two alert cat faces
on poles, as though on guard.

 Maybe her cat had died
run over by a speeding driver
on a busy street.

But no, maybe she
 lost her job in spite
of free overtime;
 not friendly enough
said the boss in a sly way.
Maybe she had applied
and failed from the start,
she looked too serious.
Only lost love could
account for all those tears;
betrayed and rejected
by a man she thought was
honourable and caring.

I wanted to lean over and say:
my dear, he was not worthy
of you, you are too good
for him; love yourself;
one day another will
love you for your virtues
and quiet beauty.
 I left, silenced
by language
and reticence.

The cats remained on guard.

Memories of an African Landscape

A green bowl held up in the African sky by shaky
hills with memories of eruptions,
millions charge the surface of the shallow land
filled with foetid slums
rich homes protected by walls of embedded glass,
palaces with hungry lions in chains.
The hills are cloaked in the blue-green of imported
eucalyptus, always regenerating,
soaking up the seasonal rain
beside a hilltop church
where lies the emperor who planted the Australians
to make a city in his image.
Every day on a highway, cracked by
constant tremors, barefoot
women bent over, seeing only the pavement
bear bundles of scented twigs
to the city to sell
for their family meal, swaying in
white shamas sails to tempt the winds
of heaven. They get
what bits they can afford
bones ache as they trudge back up the hill
Every day, big shining trucks
noisy, fill the sweet air with foul diesel fumes
roar past them, loaded with young men in black
polished boots, gleaming brass buckles,
cradling dull steel guns
laughing at tales of sexual conquests
oblivious to the exhausted women.

This scene I remember and talk about
on the radio later in Canada

how that government sells food grown
on seized lands to buy trucks and guns:
the next week, a white man Canadian
is on the radio, when asked to comment
he dismisses my image of contrast
as irrelevant simplicity:
he wants our money to help
people who have no food, no medicine,
no HIV awareness, so he
can get the Nobel Peace Prize
he so lusts for in the secret cellar of his ego,
composing his acceptance speech with plummy tones
rarely used words so people will believe this
helper of women is too intelligent
to question his mission, charity,
not change; not demilitarization,
helping women eat and care for orphans
is his only possible action.
Governments and companies
grow fat on arms deals in back rooms
hidden in the trees, near that little church
where tired women stop to pray,
are missile launchers, radar searching the sky,
stashes of machine guns for soldiers
ready to kill their brothers, sisters, on order,
children continue to suffer, disease flourishes
women will die of exhaustion
until we cease our worship at the temple
of death and profit.

The Smallest of Red Dresses

Red dresses heaped on my porch.
Tucked in those large
enough for grown women
is the smallest of dresses,
the size of a large man's hand,
red flannelette with lace trim.

Ready to send to the Unistoten,
as messages hanging in trees;
Signing the memory of loss and pain.
Blood soaked into the soil and snow;
blood red as dresses now marking
a route of violation of women
of girls when man camps
 set loose violence and lust.

Marie, a small girl in denim overalls
takes a short walk along the highway.
Her mother knows Marie
has gone to play with a friend;
her arms cradling her favourite doll,
soft and cuddly with thick
black braids just like her own.
A doll in lace trimmed red dress
her granny lovingly stitched.

At lunch time Marie's mother
walks the same way to collect Marie,
sees ripe berries and fireweed
 along the dusty roadside.
She learns too soon that
Marie had not arrived

at her friend's home.
No one has seen her.
Some one knows,
Someone in a white pickup
has stopped, sped away
in the dust of stirred gravel,
stealing a child's life,
shattering this peaceful community.
Marie's mother running home,
 running fast, running in fear,
running to call friends,
running to outrun fear,
maybe even to call distant police,
running to grasp hope that
 the day will end happy,
while deep inside knowing
as she runs, it will not.
On a shaded bend in the highway
lies Marie's doll, dirty with one arm
missing and dress torn,
glowing blood-red in the gravel.
A dress like all the others,
a flag of searing pain
and endless grief.

The smallest of red dresses
discarded like a small life;
a hand signal fluttering in the fall breeze.
Add to hundreds of other dresses
telling history from tree branches
along a pipeline route.

Art and Photo TJW.

Banner and Photo TJW.

I saw Jenin

On a calm and bright morning, I visit friends,
along a narrow alley between blocks of flats.
Their cat jumped in front to greet us
where old men sitting drinking coffee.
I saw a balcony hung with rich coloured
carpets glowing in the sunlight.
Later our friends said: they came yesterday
and occupied thar flat, locked
the women in a room- after demanding
their money and jewellery.
They took away several young men after
urinating and worse on those capers
hanging to dry after we cleaned them.
I imagined soldiers with the Star of David
surging up the alley with machine guns,
riot gear covering their stone eyes,
dehumanised by the love of brutality.
Life goes on in Jenin.

Last week another surge of soldiers
shooting as they came,
seeing the word PRESS so clearly
they knew their target immediately.
Shireen died because she would not cloak
the truth; because she, like many, she believed
that truth known would bring justice;
she made it her life work, her calling,
ignored dangers and constant threats.
A woman with a gentle soul and a big smile.

The sun shines again on Jenin.
Cats and old men
reclaim their space for now.

I saw Jenin and live to tell my story.
Shireen did not:
her story lives on in others:
the truth will set Palestine free.

Christmas in June

On a busy street in Bath,
an elegant old city,
with gracious buildings,
many expensive shops
where determined tourists
and suave locals
throng the streets.

Near an old red telephone box,
now bursting with geraniums
on a warm June day,
she parted the crowd
like Moses before the Red Sea.
Stumping along, sturdy cane
in one hand, a clutch of plastic
carrier bags in the other,
treading firmly in red velour
bedroom slippers.
Her shabby tweed skirts
had a trail of lace
petticoat hanging down
over wrinkled lisle stockings.
Cardigans piled on top of
each other; a collar and
wristbands of a green showed
under multi-coloured stripes
down to her legs, under
a comic Christmas cardigan
buttoned up, with one empty
button hole flapping
under a beaming Santa Claus.
On her head with tufts of grey hair

sticking out, she wore a red beret,
seam pulled over her ears;
topped by a pink toque
laden with bouncing pompoms.
When the crowd stopped
at the intersection's red light,
she leaned on her cane,
close by two young people
tittered and stared at her.
She glared and shook her cane.
The light changed; people scurried
across the road, she waited alone
to step out, just before
the light changed to red again,
boldly in front of waiting vehicles.
As it turned red, she paused,
nodded at the Jaguar driver,
lifted her cane in a royal salute,
then strolled slowly across
in her sturdy slippers.
Pink pompoms galore
atop of her toque danced
above her toothless smile,
dispensed to those who dared
not advance on their green.